INTERVENTION

Decodable Multi-syllable Phonics Unit

VC/V

MANUAL

© Two Pencils and a Book.
All rights reserved. © 2022 Two Pencils and a Book

ISBN 979-8370715815

Decodable Multisyllable Words Set 3

Research Based

WHY FLUENCY?

To be considered "on level" in reading fluency, students should be able to read aloud an unrehearsed passage, (i.e., either narrative or expository, fiction or non-fiction that is 200 to 300 words in length) from a grade-level text, with at least 95% accuracy in word reading. As students read aloud, their reading should sound as effortless as if they were speaking (Hasbrouck & Glaser, 2012.) This does not come easily for some students, which is why fluency practice is so essential.

In order to be considered fluent readers, students in grades 9 through 12 should be able to correctly read 150 words per minute (Hasbrouck & Tindal, 2006). In 2006 and again in 2010, Hasbrouck and Hasbrouck and Tindal (respectively) put forth that "[i]t is sufficient for students to read unpracticed, grade-level text at the 50th percentile of oral reading fluency norms" and that "...teachers do not need to have students read faster because there is no evidence that reading faster than the 50th percentile increases comprehension." See chart below.

The best strategy for developing and improving reading fluency is to provide students with many opportunities to read the same passages orally several times. These exercises provide such opportunities. On each passage, there is space for reading fluency calculations. The best part is that the passages are quick and make it easy for students to read aloud repeatedly – and often – without taking up a lot of valuable classroom time. The activities can also be spread over several days.

Grade	Percentile	Fall WPM	Winter WPM	Spring WPM	Grade	Percentile	Fall WPM	Winter WPM	Spring WPM
1	90		81	111	5	90	166	182	194
1	75		47	82	5	75	139	156	168
1	50		23	53	5	50	110	127	139
1	25		12	28	5	25	85	99	109
1	10		6	15	5	10	61	74	83
2	90	106	125	142	6	90	177	195	204
2	75	79	100	117	6	75	153	167	177
2	50	51	72	89	6	50	127	140	150
2	25	25	42	61	6	25	98	111	122
2	10	11	18	31	6	10	68	82	93
3	90	128	146	162	7	90	180	192	202
3	75	99	120	137	7	75	156	165	177
3	50	71	92	107	7	50	128	136	150
3	25	44	62	78	7	25	102	109	123
3	10	21	36	48	7	10	79	88	98
4	90	145	166	180	8	90	185	199	199
4	75	119	139	152	8	75	161	173	177
4	50	94	112	123	8	50	133	146	151
4	25	68	87	98	8	25	106	115	125
4	10	45	61	72	8	10	77	84	97

These passages are Designed for older students who are very low readers.

This programs works for resource, whole class, RTI, and summer school. If you are using this program with more than one student – partner up. Partnering students is engaging and lets everyone participate. I find that students helping students builds confidence and reinforces learning; additionally, by reading, tracking and reading again, student exposure to each passage is maximized. Research suggests that pairing readings with like-level reading partners is motivating and increases reading success.

Instruction for Group, Whole Class, or Zoom Fluency Practice

Before you begin, have a copy of one passage for each student. The PDF can be displayed before the whole class on a Smartboard or printed and projected on a document camera. As you explain the lessons, demonstrate what students will be doing.

Explain what fluency is - the rate and ease at which we read along with the flow of reading.

Break students into pairs and hand out one copy per student. If you are working with a group of students with varying abilities - pair like-leveled students together.

Explain the entire activity, as well as how to calculate combined words per minute, or CWPM. Then read the passage aloud. Have students track on their sheets as you read aloud. It is extremely beneficial for struggling students to hear the passage before they read it aloud. The goal isn't to have students stumble, but to optimize opportunities for ultimate success.

The first few times you do fluency as a class – the script below may be helpful:

1. **Check to make sure each person is in the right spot and then read the passage.**
2. **After you read the selected passage aloud, partner students and say something like:** *Put your name on your paper. Since you need to be marking your partner's paper, switch papers now. Raise your hand if you are Partner 1.*
3. **Pause until one student from each pair has their hand raised – acknowledge students when one person of each pair has their hand raised.**
4. **Raise your hand if you are Partner 2.** Pause until the other student from each pair has their hand raised – acknowledge students when the other partner has their hand raised.

   Excellent. When I say "Begin", all Partner 1s should quietly begin to read to their partners.

   All Partner 2s will use their pencils to keep track of their partner's errors. Partner 2s will put a line over each word pronounced incorrectly.

   When the timer goes off, all Partner 2s will circle the last word read, but Partner 1s will keep reading until the passage is complete. Does anyone have any questions?

5. **Set the timer for two minutes. If there are no questions** - *Begin.*
6. **When the timer goes off:** *Partner 2s, please mark your partner's score and give feedback to Partner 1s.*
7. **Walk around the room to make sure scores are being marked correctly.**
8. **Make sure students are ready and then switch for Partner 2s to read.**

   Ready? Begin.

Multisyllabic Word Reading Research

To progress in reading, students must have strategies for decoding big words. From fifth grade on, the average student encounters about 10,000 new words each year. Most of these words are multisyllabic. (Nagy and Anderson 1984).

It is helpful for students to be familiar with the common rules for syllable division. Knowing these rules and being able to apply them flexibly will help students decode longer multisyllabic words. (Carreker 2005; Henry 2010b)

According to Shefelbine and Calhoun 1991, "Low decoders, correctly pronounced fewer affixes and vowel sounds, disregarded large portions of letter information and were two to four times more likely to omit syllables."
Several studies have shown that teaching students strategies for decoding longer words improves their decoding ability. (Archer et al. 2006; Archer 2018.)

Recognizing a Decoding Problem Symptoms:
- Guesses at words from context
- Avoids sounding out new words
- Confuses similar sounds, symbols, and/or words
- Inaccurate reading of nonsense words or words out of context
- Inadequate sight word vocabulary
- Tires easily, looks away, is easily frustrated, hates to read

These strategies build word recognition and build strong readers:
- Phonemic Awareness
- Vocabulary/Morphology
- Fluency

Teaching Syllabication
- Syllabication instruction teaches a struggling reader strategies to decode multisyllable words quickly.
- Students learn to systematically break a multisyllable work into small manageable syllables, identify the vowel sounds within each syllable and "sound out" the word syllable by syllable.
- As students progress through the lessons, they will internalize the process and apply it easily and effortlessly.
- They will become faster, more efficient and fluent readers who comprehend at a higher level.

Multisyllable Words Rule: VC/V – Divide after the consonant if the first vowel has a short sound. Separate these words with the VC/V pattern.

Teacher Page

Word	Correct	Word	Correct
cabin		melon	
cricket		finish	
habit		jacket	
planet		promise	
never		radish	
robin		rocket	
seven		talent	
vanish		visit	

Student Page

Multisyllable Words Rule: VC/V – Divide after the consonant if the first vowel has a short sound. Separate these words with the V/CV pattern.

Word	Word
cabin	melon
cricket	finish
habit	jacket
planet	promise
never	radish
robin	rocket
seven	talent
vanish	visit

Multisyllable Words Rule: VC/V – Divide after the consonant if the first vowel has a short sound. Separate these words with the VC/V pattern.

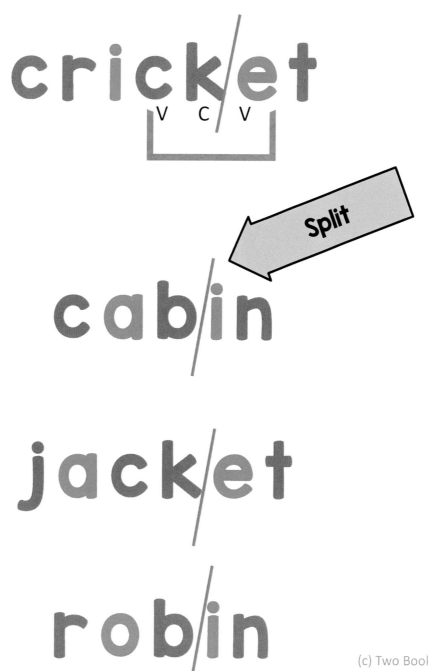

cric/et

V   C   V

Split

cab/in

jack/et

rob/in

8

cricket   jacket

cabin

jacket   robin

cricket

robin   cabin

jacket

cabin   cricket

robin

jacket   cabin

cabin

Multisyllable Words Rule: VC/V – Divide after the consonant if the first vowel has a short sound. Separate these words with the VC/V pattern.

Word Search

Find each word twice.

```
W U X B L E J C Y S J R M F P
P L A N E T E R P E X O E F I
J H L L K G V I P V R B O H E
D A A H D O I C R E O I P R A
W L C J Y L S K W N B N L V U
N W C K A N I E Y K I C A I O
C I B L E C T T Z B N A N S W
X R B L A T K Y W W D B E I S
E F I P B W J E T W I I T T E
J H K C N J A A T C H N Z J V
J A I W K M F A C N A I O P E
I W C O Q E U J Y K N B B Z N
Z S E K X G T I Z B E M I X P
G G S Y E H F Q B S C T F N J
C H B W P T D E E W I L U I I
```

Word Bank:
cricket
robin
cabin
jacket
planet
seven
jacket
visit

Write two sentences using: cricket, cabin, jacket, and robin.

_____

_____

_____

_____

_____

_____

_____

_____

ACROSS

3. a pretty red bird

6. Put on your ____. It's cold outside.

7. between five and six

DOWN

1. a small house

2. an insect that chirps

4. We live on ____ earth.

5. We will ____ grandma for her birthday.

Sentence Fluency: VC/V – cricket, cabin, jacket, robin

Pack your jacket.	06
Pack your jacket for the cabin.	11
We are going to the cabin.	18
We are going to the cabin, so we need to pack our jackets.	29
The cabin is in the forest.	34
The cabin is by a lake in the forest.	43
There are crickets at the cabin.	54
There are crickets at the cabin by the lake.	59
There are not crickets in the cabin.	65
There are crickets by the cabin.	73
There are also robins by the cabin.	78
There are crickets and robins by the cabin.	86
We will look for robins.	93
We will look for robins by the cabin.	99
We will have to wear our jackets.	112
We will wear our jackets when we look for robins.	124
We will hike near the cabin.	130
We will hike near the cabin to look for robins.	141
We will sit by the lake at the cabin.	149
We will sit by the lake, by the cabin, to listen for crickets.	155
We will wear our jackets when we listen for crickets.	164
We will have fun looking for crickets and robins at the cabin.	170

Words Read: _____ minus mistakes: _____ equals wpms: _____	Words Read: _____ minus mistakes: _____ equals wpms: _____	Words Read: _____ minus mistakes: _____ equals wpms: _____
Words Read: _____ minus mistakes: _____ equals wpms: _____	Words Read: _____ minus mistakes: _____ equals wpms: _____	Words Read: _____ minus mistakes: _____ equals wpms: _____

Fluency: VC/V – cricket, cabin, jacket, robin

"Grab your hats and jackets. We are going to the cabin!" Mom called down	14
the hall.	16
"Do you know where my cricket net is?" Johnny called from his room.	29
"It's by the robin food on the table," Dad said.	39
Johnny ran out of his room. He was wearing his backpack. He did not have	54
his jacket.	56
"Jacket?" Dad asked.	59
"Jacket. Right." Johnny turned back around. He grabbed his jacket.	69
"Put your things by the door. I'll put them in the car," Mom said.	83
"I'll grab the cricket net and robin food from the kitchen," Johnny said.	96
"You know catching crickets is back luck," Maria said. Maria was Johnny's	108
little sister.	110
"Not if you let them go after you look at them. Did you get your jacket?"	126
Johnny asked. He was a great big brother.	134
"Jacket," Maria said running back to the closet. "I better take two. I get	148
pretty dirty at the cabin."	153
"All aboard," Mom called from outside. "The robins, crickets, and cabin are	165
waiting."	166

Words Read: _____ minus mistakes: _____ equals wpms: _____	Words Read: _____ minus mistakes: _____ equals wpms: _____	Words Read: _____ minus mistakes: _____ equals wpms: _____
Words Read: _____ minus mistakes: _____ equals wpms: _____	Words Read: _____ minus mistakes: _____ equals wpms: _____	Words Read: _____ minus mistakes: _____ equals wpms: _____

Directions: Please select the best response.

1. From the reading, I can infer Johnny
   a. likes school
   b. likes animals
   c. eats crickets
   d. likes to catch crickets

2. Who had to run back for their jacket?
   a. Maria
   b. Tommy
   c. Mom
   d. Dad

3. Where is the family going?
   a. grandmother's house
   b. skiing
   c. a hotel
   d. a cabin

4. What was Johnny wearing when he came out of his room?
   a. a hat
   b. a jacket
   c. a backpack
   d. a bug catching net

5. Where were the cricket net and robin food?
   a. the porch
   b. the lawn
   c. the kitchen
   d. Johnny's bedroom

6. "Johnny was a ____ big brother."
   a. good
   b. funny
   c. playful
   d. loving

7. Put a line through the syllable break.

Example: ca/bin

c r i c k e t

c a   b i n

r o b i n

j a c k e t

c h i c k e n

t a l e n t

8. VC/V – Rewrite the rule in your own words:

Multisyllable Words Rule 3: VC/V – Divide after the consonant if the first vowel has a short sound.

_____

_____

_____

_____

_____

_____

_____

_____

_____

Instructions: Cut along the solid lines. Fold along the dotted lines. Color and decorate. Paste in your interactive notebook.

robin   cricket   cabin

jacket

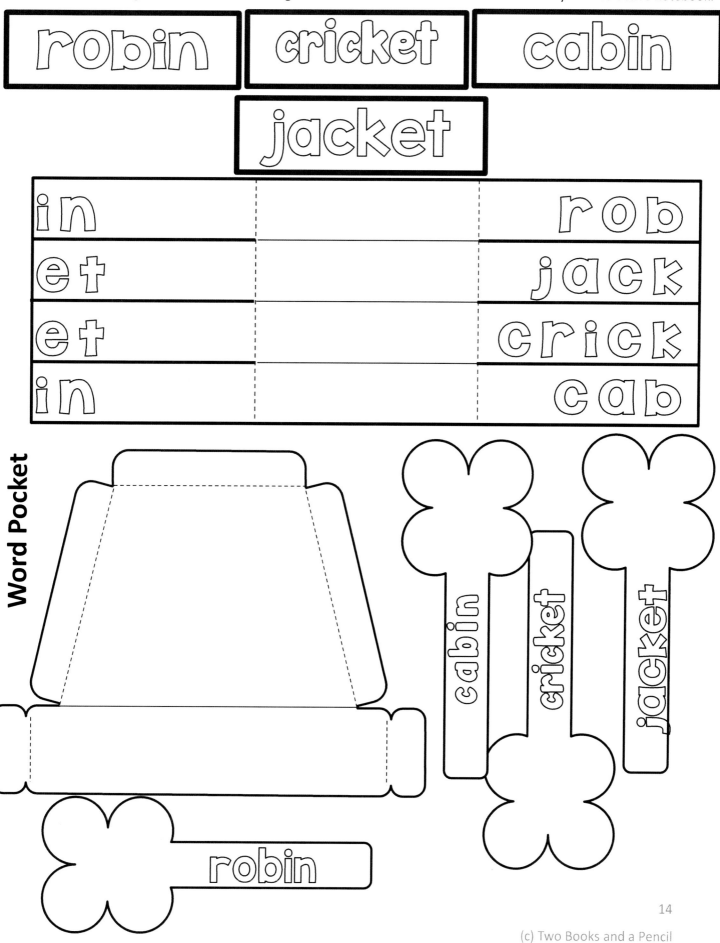

in		rob
et		jack
et		crick
in		cab

Word Pocket

cabin   cricket   jacket

robin

VC/V

Multisyllable Words Rule: VC/V – Divide after the consonant if the first vowel has a short sound. Separate these words with the VC/V pattern. 1.

plan/et

seven

Split

rock/et

vis/it

planet

visit

rocket

seven

visit

visit

rocket

seven

planet

rocket

visit

seven

16

Multisyllable Words Rule 3: VC/V – Divide after the consonant if the first vowel has a short sound. Separate these words with the VC/V pattern.

Directions: Find Each Word Twice

Word Search

```
E R O C K E T D W R P I R J U
K Z J S Y K P G W X H E J A L
E P V F H W N L S E V E N C M
C K Y W B Q G C A A B M A K X
R O G C A B I N P N Z N W E G
I P C R I C K E T J E P K T H
C P O P R F D S R P A T T C Q
K L Y G P A M P O A L C X K X
E N R F O V R O B I N A K S Z
T P Z P B L I D I O N D N E C
Z A B T S E V E N C W J Z E T
C A B I N S P C B I I D A J T
M X U V I S I T E J I N A L Z
P C H D C P Q R O C K E T L M
Y U S U E Q V I S I T S R M H
```

Word Bank:
cricket
jacket
cabin
robin
planet
seven
rocket
visit

ACROSS

2. to go and spend time with someone
4. something you wear over your clothes
5. you would take one if you want to go to space
7. five, six, ____, eight

DOWN

1. a small insect
3. we live on one
5. a bird that usually has a red breast
6. a small house

17

(c) Two Books and a Pencil

Sentence Fluency: VC/V– planet, seven, rocket, visit

The earth is a planet.	05
Mars is a planet.	09
Saturn is also a planet.	14
No one ever visits Saturn.	19
If you want to visit a plant, you need to take a rocket.	32
To visit the planet Mars, you must take a rocket.	42
Devon wants to be an astronaut.	48
Devon wants to visit Mars.	50
Devon wants to visit Mars and seven other planets.	57
Which planets does Devon want to visit?	64
Mars, we know he wants to visit Mars.	72
He also wants to visit the planet Jupiter.	80
Kyle discovered a solar system with seven planets.	88
He is building a rocket to fly to all seven planets.	99
He has to build a powerful rocket to get to all seven.	111
He could build seven rockets.	116
If he built seven rockets, he could visit them one at a time.	129
It would take a long time to visit seven planets.	139
It would take a long time to build seven rockets.	149

Words Read: _____ minus mistakes: _____ equals wpms: _____	Words Read: _____ minus mistakes: _____ equals wpms: _____	Words Read: _____ minus mistakes: _____ equals wpms: _____
Words Read: _____ minus mistakes: _____ equals wpms: _____	Words Read: _____ minus mistakes: _____ equals wpms: _____	Words Read: _____ minus mistakes: _____ equals wpms: _____

Fluency: VC/V – planet, seven, rocket, visit

"It's a letter and a box from NASA. I'm so nervous," Ava said.	13
Ava was a grad student. She was studying the planets. She applied for a	27
special program. The program was for seven people to take a rocket to Mars.	41
The box and the letter were a good sign. If she wasn't accepted, she	55
probably would have just gotten an email.	62
"Open them!" Ollie said. Ollie was Ava's roommate. She knew how long Ava	75
had been waiting. She also know how badly Ava wanted to visit other planets.	89
"I'm going to the planet Mars!" Ava said.	97
"You were picked? You were picked to be one of the seven?" Ollie asked.	111
"I was picked as one of the seven to visit the planet Mars!"	124
"Wow! Thousands applied to visit the planet Mars."	132
"And I get to go. I will have seven months of training," Ava said.	146
"Do you get to go in that underwater training cabin?" Ollie asked.	158
"I guess. The program is to get us planet ready."	168
"What is in the box?" Ollie asked.	175
"It's my rocket jacket. Isn't it cool!" Ava put on the jacket. She spun around.	190
"Actually, it is my training jacket."	196
"I love the design. I love the seven dots around Mars."	207
"They stand for each one of us." Ava plopped down on the couch. "I can't	222
believe I get to visit another planet."	229
"You are a rock star! I'm so proud of you."	239
"I have to go call my mom!"	246

Words Read: _____ minus mistakes: _____ equals wpms: _____	Words Read: _____ minus mistakes: _____ equals wpms: _____	Words Read: _____ minus mistakes: _____ equals wpms: _____
Words Read: _____ minus mistakes: _____ equals wpms: _____	Words Read: _____ minus mistakes: _____ equals wpms: _____	Words Read: _____ minus mistakes: _____ equals wpms: _____

Directions: Please select the best response.

1. Who is the box and the letter from?
    a.   her mom
    b.   Ollie
    c.   SpaceX
    d.   NASA

2. Where is Ava going?
    a.   Jupiter
    b.   Saturn
    c.   Mars
    d.   the moon

3.   Why are there seven dots on the logo?
    a.   for seven planets they are traveling to
    b.   for the seven people selected to go to Saturn
    c.   for the seven people selected to go to Mars
    d.   because seven is a lucky number

4.   How many people applied to go to Mars?
    a.   seven
    b.   100s
    c.   1000s
    d.   exactly one thousand

5.   Ava put on the _____ and spun around.
    a.   shirt
    b.   hat
    c.   coat
    d.   jacket

6.   Put the statements in the order in which they occur in the reading.
    a.   Ava put on the jacket
    b.   Ava opened the box
    c.   Ava found out she won
    d.   Ava said she was nervous

    _____   _____   _____   _____

7. Put a line through the syllable break.

Example: cab/in

c r i c k e t

c a b i n

r o b i n

j a c k e t

v i s i t

p l a n e t

c a b i n

s e v e n

visit	planet	rocket

seven		

en		sev
et		rock
it		vis
et		plan

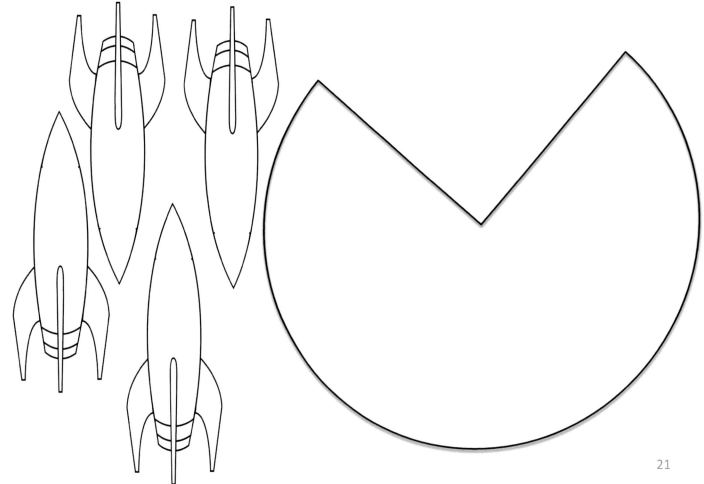

Our Solar System

Our solar system is made up of our star, the Sun, and everything that orbits it. Orbit just means to travel around it.

The planets in our Solar System are Mercury, Venus, Earth, Mars, Jupiter, Saturn, Uranus, and Neptune. There are also dwarf planets like Pluto. Plus, dozens of moons, and millions of asteroids, comets, and meteoroids. Beyond our solar system, there are thousands of planetary systems orbiting other stars in the Milky Way.

Things to Know About Our Solar System

- Our solar system orbits the center of the galaxy. Our galaxy is the Milky Way. It orbits at about 515,000 miles per hour.
- We are one of the galaxy's four spiral arms.
- It takes the solar system about 230 million years to make one orbit around the center of the galaxy.
- There are three kinds of galaxies: elliptical, spiral, and irregular.
- The Milky Way is a spiral galaxy.
- The planets of our solar system have over 200 moons in their orbits.
- More than 300 robot spacecraft have explored outside of Earth's orbit.
- Twenty-four US Astronauts have made the trip from the Earth to the moon.
- The Solar System formed 4.6 billion years ago.
- The Sun is 93 millions miles away from the earth.
- Neptune was the last planet of the Solar System be discovered.
- You'd need 18 Mercuries to be the same size as the earth.
- All of the planets are named after Roman and Greek gods except Earth.
- Earth means ground.
- Mars is cold and dry.
- But Mars does have water in the form of ice.

22

Our Solar System
Informational Posts

Use the information from the reading and the VC/C words to create two Instagram posts below the photos.

♡ ◯ ▽   🔖

comment

♡ ◯ ▽   🔖

comment

Multisyllable Words Rule: VC/V – Divide after the consonant if the first vowel has a short sound. Separate these words with the VC/V pattern.

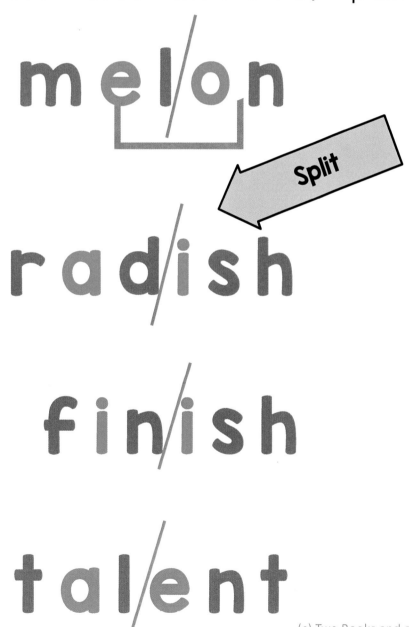

melon

finish

radish

talent

melon

radish

finish

melon

talent

talent

radish

melon

Multisyllable Words Rule 3: VC/V – Divide after the consonant if the first vowel has a short sound. Separate these words with the VC/V pattern.

Word Search

D A O U Q H U V T T S I H J U
H T E W Y P I S R R A E F W W
S C K O O J U I R E A L C L G
P V R T C S A V L N N D E H T
G R A I Y N F E E F Q Q I N G
T O O T C W J O N E S Y T S T
C C P C T K X C D F E P R U H
L M L T K H E C L J V N M C Y
R M A K P E X T A T E X E C X
O N N X K P T P P B N I L Q O
B H E X V K U D P W I F O Q Q
I M T Q Y Q W B K F R N N Z I
N S C J A C K E T E L K H P J
H E Q E M V E S Y L Z X G Y C
Z Q F I N I S H U V I S I T A

Word Bank:
cricket
jacket
cabin
robin
planet
seven
rocket
visit
melon
radish
finish
talent

Write two sentences using: melon, radish, finish, and talent.

_____

_____

_____

_____

_____

_____

_____

_____

_____

_____

Across
2. Mars is one of them
6. a small insect
7. a number between 5 and 6
9. an edible root, usually red
10. Cantaloupe is one of them

Down
1. you wear it over your clothes
3. a natural skill
4. you use it to get to space
5. Did he cross the ___ line first?
8. We are going to ___grandmother
9. a bird with a red breast.

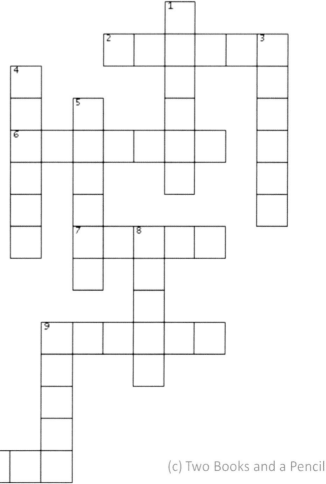

Sentence Fluency: VC/V – melon, radish, finish, talent

He has so much talent.	05
Chef Bobby has talent making radish salad.	12
Chef Bobby has talent making radish and melon salad.	21
He starts by cutting up radishes.	27
He digs the melon out with a melon ball tool.	37
He arranges them neatly on a platter.	44
He finishes it off with a splatter of rice vinegar.	54
It is a delicious radish salad when it is all finished.	65
There are so many things such a talented chef can do.	76
Chef Bobby's restaurant is farm to table.	83
He grows his own radishes and melons.	90
He grows many other types of melons.	97
He makes many wonderful dishes out of his vegetables.	106
The people in his restaurant love his talent.	114
The people in his restaurant love his talent and finish ever last bite.	127
Chef Bobby also makes a melon spaghetti.	134
He picks the melon before it is ripe.	142
He cuts the melon open, and he strings it.	151
The melon really looks like spaghetti.	157
It tastes like spaghetti too.	162
He is very talent**ed.**	166
Chef Bobby can do anything with radishes and melon.	175

Words Read: _____ minus mistakes: _____ equals wpms: _____	Words Read: _____ minus mistakes: _____ equals wpms: _____	Words Read: _____ minus mistakes: _____ equals wpms: _____
Words Read: _____ minus mistakes: _____ equals wpms: _____	Words Read: _____ minus mistakes: _____ equals wpms: _____	Words Read: _____ minus mistakes: _____ equals wpms: _____

Fluency: VC/V – melon, radish, finish, talent

"I can't wait to visit the **Beat Bobby Flay** set. He's so talented," Dustin said.	15
"Will we get to see it taped?" Rena asked.	24
"Yep, and his guests are Anne and Giada."	32
"Cool. That'll make it extra fun."	38
They got to the studio early. They sat in the front row. They were right above	54
the kitchen on Bobby's side.	59
The lights flickered. The warm-up guy pointed to the applause sign. The girls	73
cheered. The crowd was on its feet. The talented Bobby Flay came out. He	87
introduced the first-round judges. He introduced the chef contestants.	97
"The ingredients you are going to cook with are seven radishes and casaba	110
melon."	111
"Those are tough," Dustin said.	116
"I'd go melon and radish salad," Rena said.	124
Giada walked over to one of the cook stations. "What are you making	137
chef?"	138
"Cucumber, melon, and radish salad with a serrano vinaigrette," he said.	149
"How about you? Is that bacon?" She asked the other chef.	160
"Takes no talent to add bacon," the first chef teased. "Now prosciutto…"	172
"The perfect pairing with melon."	177
Dustin leaned forward. "Bacon guy's gonna pull it off - watch."	187
Bacon guy made the best use of melon and radishes, but he could not beat	202
Bobby Flay.	203
"What a fun day!" Rena said. "What talented chefs."	212
"It made me hungry. Let's get a melon and radish salad on the way home."	227

Words Read: _____ minus mistakes: _____ equals wpms: _____	Words Read: _____ minus mistakes: _____ equals wpms: _____	Words Read: _____ minus mistakes: _____ equals wpms: _____
Words Read: _____ minus mistakes: _____ equals wpms: _____	Words Read: _____ minus mistakes: _____ equals wpms: _____	Words Read: _____ minus mistakes: _____ equals wpms: _____

Directions: Please select the best response.

1. What show did the Dustin and Rena go see?
    a.   Bobby Flay
    b.   Beat Bobby
    c.   Bobby and Giada
    d.   Beat Bobby Flay

2. What ingredients does Bobby assign
    a.   serrano peppers
    b.   peppers and melon
    c.   radishes and peppers
    d.   melon and radishes

3. Who won in the end?
    a.   Dustin
    b.   Giada
    c.   Bobby Flay
    d.   Bacon guy

4. Who does Dustin say will be the guest judges?
    a.   Bobby and Giada
    b.   Anne and Bobby
    c.   Giada and Bobby
    d.   Anne and Giada

5. What kind of melon is mentioned in the passage?
    a.   watermelon
    b.   cucumber melon
    c.   cantaloupe melon
    d.   casaba melon

6. Put the statements in the order they appear in the reading
    a.   Dustin and Rena go eat
    b.   they sit in the front row
    c.   Bacon guy wins the first round
    d.   Bobby Flay comes on the set

_____ _____ _____ _____

7. Put a line through the syllable break.

Example: cab/in

melon

radish

finish

talent

cricket

cabin

robin

jacket

visit

planet

cabin

seven

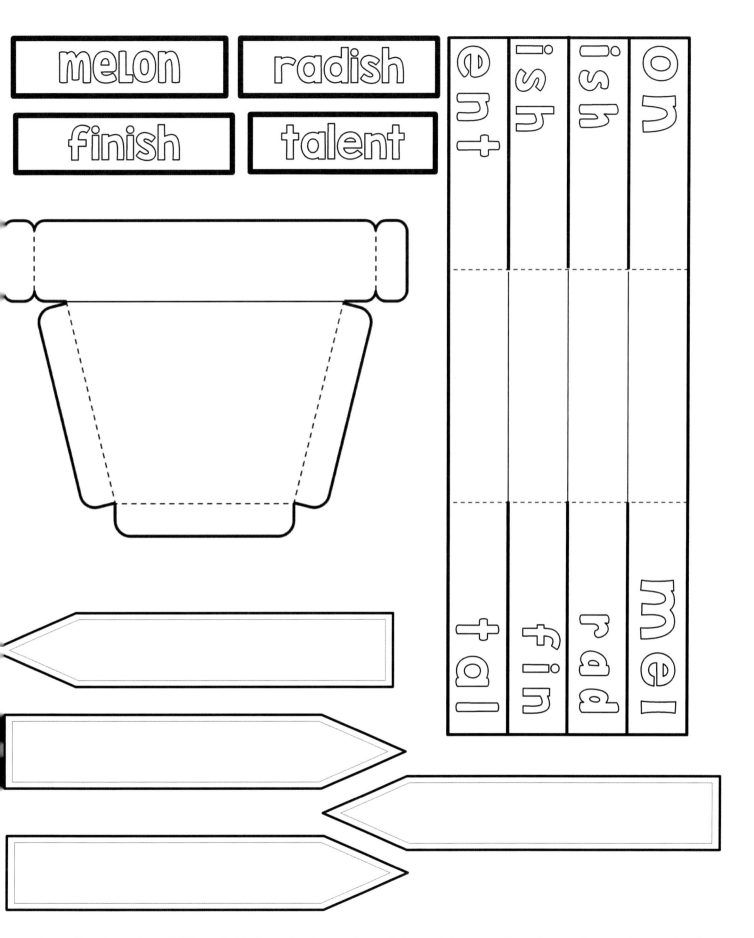

melon

radish

finish

talent

ent

ish

ish

on

tal

fin

rad

mel

Instructions: Cut along the solid lines. Fold along the dotted lines. Color and decorate. Paste in your interactive notebook.

30

VC/V

Multisyllable Words Rule: VC/V – Divide after the consonant if the first vowel has a short sound. Separate these words with the VC/V pattern.

never   vanish

habit   never

habit

habit

never

vanish

habit

never

habit   vanish

Multisyllable Words Rule: VC/V – Divide after the consonant if the first vowel has a short sound. Separate these words with the VC/C pattern.

Write two sentences using: habit, vanish, and never.

_____

_____

_____

_____

_____

_____

_____

Word Search

```
O N K G D T S H C A B I N V O
N L B H A B I T W Z P I O A O
S C I R B M H U F W L L H N X
N E R A U M N A F V A G L I N
M D V I F U E E Z J N R S S F
W K K E C M N L R M E B N H I
C Q U R N K M T O Z T C E J N
B I G J U I E L C N W S V R I
R M C A F B Z T K T U N E A S
O N P C P K D M E T O I R D H
B U F K A R D L T Y H J L I V
I W I E G I W N X N R O S S T
N A X T X G H J B K D S T H A
R E W A V I S I T T A L E N T
K G W O Z I N P C A W J G T Z
```

Word Bank:
cricket
jacket
cabin
robin
planet
seven
rocket
visit
melon
radish
finish
talent
habit
vanish
never

ACROSS
4. We will stay in a ____ by the lake.
6. Put on your ____ before you go outside.
7. The magician made the ball ____ into thin air.
9. We'll take a ____ to the moon.
10. There were ____ brides for seven brothers.
11. We will ____ the moon on a rocket.
13. I will ____ jump out of an airplane.
14. We reached the ___ at the same time.

DOWN
1. The ____ were chirping loudly.
2. The ____ ate out of the bird feeder.
3. The ____ earth could really use our help.
5. Biting your nails is a ____ habit.
8. The water____ was sweet and juicy.
9. The red ____ grew in the ground.
12. Kobe Bryant had so much ____.

Sentence Fluency: VC/V – habit, never, vanish

Biting your nails is a bad habit.	07
You should never bite your nails.	13
It is a bad habit to bite your nails.	22
You should never say never.	27
You should never say never again.	33
Walking is a good habit.	38
Smiling is a good habit.	43
Being kind is a good habit.	49
The magician made the rabbit vanish.	55
He pulled it out of his hat, and then he made the rabbit vanish.	69
I never want to stop caring.	75
I never want you to stop caring.	82
Caring can't vanish from the earth.	88
How do you break a bad habit?	95
You replace it with a good habit.	102
Your bad habits will vanish if you replace them with good habits.	114
Joe says he has no bad habits.	121
He practiced good habits, and his bad habits vanished.	130
I say one bad habit did not vanish.	138
What bad habit hasn't vanished?	143
The bad habit that did not vanish is that he brags about not having bad habits.	159

Words Read: _____ minus mistakes: _____ equals wpms: _____	Words Read: _____ minus mistakes: _____ equals wpms: _____	Words Read: _____ minus mistakes: _____ equals wpms: _____
Words Read: _____ minus mistakes: _____ equals wpms: _____	Words Read: _____ minus mistakes: _____ equals wpms: _____	Words Read: _____ minus mistakes: _____ equals wpms: _____

Fluency: VC/V – habit, never, vanish

"I've decided I'm not going to bite my nails anymore. It's a bad habit," Tita	15
told her mom.	18
"Good idea. Your orthodontist will thank you," Mom said.	27
"I should never have started to begin with. It's easier to not start a habit, than	43
to break a habit."	47
"I read that it takes about 21 days to break a bad habit," Mom said.	62
"I don't have 21 days. Prom is in six days. I really want pretty nails for prom,"	79
Tita said.	81
"We'll get you acrylics," Mom said.	87
"That'd be cool, but they'll probably taste awful!" Tita said.	97
"You won't be biting your nails. Remember? You're breaking that habit,"	108
Mom said.	110
"Well, if I get acrylics, I won't need to break my habit."	122
Mom rolled her eyes as Tita's little sister, Emmie, skipped into the room.	135
"What to see me make this rabbit vanish?" she asked her mom and sister.	149
"How 'bout you vanish squirt?" Tita teased.	156
"Of course we do," Mom said.	162
"This has never worked before, but here goes nothing." Emmie showed them	174
the empty hat. She waved a wand over it. Put in a stuffed rabbit. "Presto," she	190
said.	191
She looked in the hat and the rabbit was gone.	201
"I did it!" she squealed.	206
"Great!" Tita said. "Now, make my nail-biting habit disappear."	216

Words Read: _____ minus mistakes: _____ equals wpms: _____	Words Read: _____ minus mistakes: _____ equals wpms: _____	Words Read: _____ minus mistakes: _____ equals wpms: _____
Words Read: _____ minus mistakes: _____ equals wpms: _____	Words Read: _____ minus mistakes: _____ equals wpms: _____	Words Read: _____ minus mistakes: _____ equals wpms: _____

VC/V habit, never, vanish

Directions: Please select the best response.

1. What habit does Tita want to break?
    - a.   putting her elbows on the table
    - b.   going to bed too late
    - c.   biting her nails
    - d.   teasing people

2. Why does Tita want nice nails?
    - a.   all her friends have them
    - b.   homecoming is coming
    - c.   prom is coming
    - d.   she is tired of not having nice things

3. What did Emmie make vanish?
    - a.   a hat
    - b.   a wand
    - c.   a bunny
    - d.   a rabbit

4. Why does Tita decide she may not have to break her bad habit?
    - a.   she will wear gloves
    - b.   she'll get acrylics
    - c.   she won't go
    - d.   she will hide her hands.

5. Who skipped into the room?
    - a.   Mom
    - b.   Emmie
    - c.   Tita
    - d.   Emily

6. Put the statements in the order in which they appear in the reading.
    - a.   Tita decides to break a bad habit
    - b.   Emmie makes something vanish
    - c.   Mom suggests acrylics
    - d.   Emmie skips into the room

_____ _____ _____ _____

7. Put a line through the syllable break.

Example: cab/in

h a b i t

n e v e r

v a n i s h

t a l e n t

c r i c k e t

c a b i n

r o b i n

j a c k e t

v i s i t

p l a n e t

c a b i n

s e v e n

Instructions: Cut along the solid lines. Fold along the dotted lines. Color and decorate. Paste in your interactive notebook.

vanish | habit | never

ER
IT
ISH

NEV
HAB
VAN

word pocket

Write a Paragraph
TOPIC: Explain a VC/V

Topic Sentence:	The topic tells the reader what the paragraph is about. **SAMPLE:** For words with a vowel-consonant-vowel pattern, divide after the consonant if the first vowel has a short. **HING:** For this essay, you may use the sample topic sentence.
Body:	The body of your paragraph provides support for your topic.
Closing Sentence:	The closing sentence refers back to the main idea. It also offers a final point about your topic.

_____

_____

_____

_____

_____

_____

_____

_____

_____

_____

_____

_____

_____

_____

_____

page 10:

```
W U X B L E J C Y S J R M F P
P L A N E T E R P E X O E F I
J H L L K G V I P V R B O H E
D A A H D O I C R E O P R A U
W L C J Y L S K W N B N L V U
N W C K A N I E Y K I C A I O
C I B L E C T T Z B N A N S W
X R B L A T K Y W W D B E I S
E F I P B W J E T W I I T T E
J H K C N J A A T C H N Z J V
J A I W K M F A C N A I O P E
I W C O Q E U J Y K N B B Z N
Z S E K X G T I Z B E M I X P
G G S Y E H F Q B S C T F N J
C H B W P T D E E W I L U I I
```

page 17:

```
E R O C K E T D W R P I R J U
K Z J S Y K P G W X H E J A L
E P V F H W N L S E V E N C M
C K Y W B Q G C A A B M A K X
R O G C A B I N P N Z N W E G
I P C R I C K E T J E P K T H
C P O P R F D S R P A T T C Q
K L Y G P A M P O A L C X K X
E N R F O V R O B I N A K S Z
T P Z P B L I D I O N D N E C
Z A B T S E V E N C W J Z E T
C A B I N S P C B I I D A J T
M X U V I S I T E J I N A L Z
P C H D C P Q R O C K E T L M
Y U S U E Q V I S I T S R M H
```

page 26:

```
D A O U Q H U V T S I H J U
H T E W Y P I S R A E F W W
S C K O O J U I R E A L C L G
P V R T C S A V L N N D E H T
G R A I Y N F E E F Q Q I N G
T O O T C W J O N E S Y T S T
C C P C T K X C D F E P R U H
L M L T K H E C L J V N M C Y
R M A K P E X T A T E X E C X
O N N X K P T P P B N I L Q O
B H E X V K U D P W I F O Q Q
I M T Q Y Q W B K F R N N Z I
N S C J A C K E T E L K H P J
H E Q E M V E S Y L Z X G Y C
Z Q F I N I S H U V I S I T A
```

page 29:

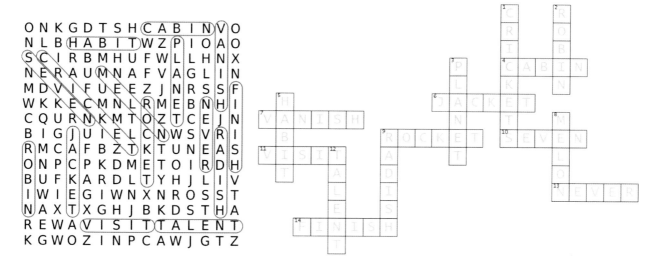

Multiple Choice Answers

page 13 1. c; 2. a; 3. d; 4. c; 5. d; 6. a

page 20 - 1. d; 2. c; 3. c; 4. c; 5. d; 6. dbca

page 29 - 1. d; 2. d; 3. a; 4. d; 5. d; 6. bdca

page 36: 1. c; 2. c; 3. d; 4. b; 5. b; 6. acdb

Thank you for your purchase. If you have any questions, please email me at nonnieshome@gmail.com.

Please look at my other products at: https://www.teacherspayteachers.com/Store/Tw

o-Pencils-And-A-Book

Theresa ☺

Credits - Clip art and fonts by:

Made in the USA
Las Vegas, NV
09 March 2024

86946569R00026